KINDLE FIRE HD

SET UP

Step by Step Manual for Starters on How to Setup a Kindle Fire HD

BY

FREDRICK M. MCCLAIN

Copyright©2018

COPYRIGHT

TABLE OF CONTENT

CHAPTER 1

INTRODUCTION

Among the most used Android devices in the world, in recent times is The Kindle Fire HD. It is estimated to have over 3 million users worldwide.

One of the features of the Kindle Fire device is its been use as an E-reader, but that doesn't mean that its functions are limited to just that. It has been noticed from findings and through wide usage that it has a very friendly user interface unlike some and it has packed in it many wonderful packages.

This work is intended to give you easy step by step procedures on how you can setup your Kindle Fire, and all that is required of you now is just follow the steps as instructed.

There are numerous Apps from other sources that can also be setup in your Kindle Fire

Tablet, notwithstanding if you find any of these difficult, there is no needs to worry as this book will help.

The challenge faced by many in setting up this all important device prompted this book and it has so far proven useful and beneficial

Thankfully the steps are easy and simple to follow, that even a starter can master it in no time.

CHAPTER 2

HOW TO SETUP YOUR KINDLE FIRE HD

The device Kindle Fire HD, which is also known as the Fire HD, is from Amazon's line of Touch Screen Tablet computers. Some of the noticeable differences are the processors, screen sizes, and other features; depending on the year of production for your Fire HD, these devices can be used also for jobs, travel, designs, etc. But its overall functions and basic work always remain unchanged.

After purchase and before activating, using or setup your Fire HD Apps to browser, read, view emails and other functionalities, you must first register Kindle Amazon using the internet.

To easily do these and more do the following:

Connect to the Internet:

1. Charge your Kindle battery:

Some power adapters for Kindle are sold separately, it has been noticed that they could charge your Fire HD faster than a USB cable, usually your Kindle would come with a USB cable which will enable you connect your new device to a computer or a USB charging port to enable charging.

Steps to charge your Fire HD:
→Get USB charger connected into your Kindle device.
→Plug USB into a power adapter, or USB port.
→Wait until your Kindle shows it's fully charged and this when the orange charging light turns green.

2. After fully charged, access the Welcome wireless connection screen:

Press the power button at the bottom of your Fire HD to turn it on and you will see:

→A slide bar; tap, hold and drag right to enable you unlock your Kindle.

→A 'welcome' note, then available Wi-Fi networks; type your password and tap the OK button when you have selected your preferred network.

3. Wi-Fi setting:

If you wish to obtain a new Wi-Fi network, move your finger from top of the screen downwards, then enter the network name and password to access it.

4. TO troubleshoot Wi-Fi problems, if necessary:

It is advisable to contact your internet provider if other devices can access your wireless network but your Kindle device can't. Follow these steps to fix common connectivity problems first:

→Turn the Airplane mode off by dragging your finger from the top of your screen to the bottom, then click the "wireless" option, and click "Off" if Airplane mode is turn on.

→To reset Wi-Fi connection all you should to do is move your finger on the screen top down, select wireless — Wi-Fi —Off. Then tap "On".

→To restart your Fire HD device, tap the power button and hold it, Remove your finger immediately it starts. You can press the power button again to set it on if Fire HD doesn't restart automatically.

→If you still are unable to access your network amongst other networks, just position your Kindle device close to the router and select wireless → Wi-Fi, then tap "Scan".

CHAPTER 3

HOW TO CONNECT TO YOUR AMAZON

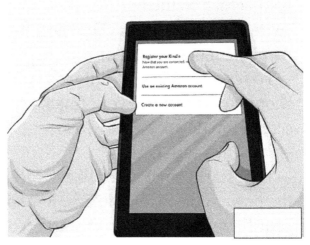

1. Continue your Kindle page registration:

After connecting your Kindle device to your wireless network, 'Kindle page Registration' should be prompted to appear on your device screen. On this page you should see the following:

→ 'Enter Amazon Account
Information.'
→Password and email entry boxes
should appear on the same page
displayed.

2. Input your Amazon account information or create an account (sign up):

If you already have an Amazon
account to proceed with the Fire HD,
type your email and password. But if
you do not have an account; enter
create account towards the bottom of
the screen.

→failure to register your Kindle account, you will be not be able to access, purchase, or receive items through Amazon's Kindle store.
→ To be able to buy content from Amazon store, you will need to link your Amazon account to your preferred source of payment. Your credit card information for your Amazon account will be needed at this point.

3. Agreeing to terms and conditions:

Select 'Register' after reading through
the terms and condition for using
Kindle Fire HD and agreeing to it.

Confirm your time zone

4. Your present time zone should be set:

A page should appear with a heading
'Select Your Time Zone' after
registration with list of other time
zones in the USA. At the bottom of
the screen, select 'More' if you live in

another country to select your
country time zone.

5. Confirm your account:

If accidentally you entered wrong
Account information instead of your
account information, click the link
provided to input and confirm your
account.

6. Get your Kindle account link to your social media:

Link your Kindle account to social media like Facebook, Instagram and twitter (optionally).
To do this simply:
→ Select your desired social media.
→ Input your correct account information, such as your email and password.
→Tap, 'Get Started Now'

7. With the tutorial provided, acquaint yourself with Fire HD:

Using the tutorial, you can get acquainted with Fire HD features of your new Kindle device. This can be done by scrolling to the user's guide in your Kindle Fire HD Docs library.

CHAPTER 4

HOW TO MAKE USE OF YOUR KINDLE FIRE HD

1. If you want, change the language settings:

To change your language setting, this can be done by moving your finger downward from the top of your screen. This should show a menu containing 'Settings.' Tap this and follow these steps:

→ Tap 'Keyboard and Language' from the options listed there.

→Select 'Language' option.

→Choose your language from the resulting list of languages provided.

→From the 'Language and Keyboard' menu change your keyboard language by tapping 'Current Keyboard'. After that, select 'Keyboard Language' on your device.

→'Use System Language', and manually select your device keyboard.

→Select 'Fire Keyboard' to choose your desire language if need to download a new keyboard for your language on your device.

2. How to manage billing settings and account information:

Unlock your Kindle Fire HD by swiping your finger or inputting your password; remove your Kindle Fire HD from sleep mode by tapping the button at the bottom of your Kindle.

From your home screen:

→ Choose 'Manage Your Content and Devices.'

→Under the 'Digital Payment Settings' option in your device, choose the option 'Edit Payment Method.'

→Next thing to do is to make adjustment on your device, enter your new payment information or your current payment method.

→After complete update of your information, Select 'Continue.'

→ When your Kindle device redirects you to the 'Digital Payment Settings' page, confirm your information is correct.

3. Search the library for eBooks and other media already purchased:

Tap the Home icon on your Kindle device to turn to the home screen, which should contain your content libraries. It is an icon with the shape little house.

→ Now all you need to do is select your desired content library to open your library of eBooks; but if you just setup your Amazon account, your content libraries will be totally and completely empty.

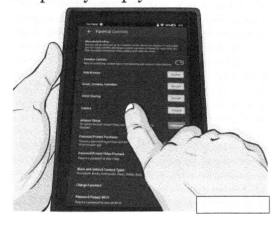

4. Set parental controls for Kindle devices used by children:

When you swipe your device down from the top of the screen, it will open your settings, there should be a 'More' option. Tap it, then tap 'Parental Settings' then:

→ Parental control settings for the Kindle Fire HD, tap the 'On', which will prompt a request for a password. Type in the password and confirm parental control password.

→ Next, after the category of features appear that you can restrict; Select 'On' for each feature that you wish restricted. Then tap on 'Finish.'

→ To show Parental Controls are enabled, you will see a small lock icon on the top status of your Kindle.

5. How to change default search engine:

Should you prefer a different browser, such as Yahoo or Google, you can change it through your menu options. Enter your browser by selecting "Web" from the home screen, and then tap the menu icon represented by three vertical dots.

→Select 'search engine' by scrolling to the 'Settings' option.

→ Chose the search engine of your choice.

→ Then you may start browsing websites with your Kindle Fire device.

6. Email setup:

From the home page, select the house icon displayed. Thereafter you may select 'Apps' and select the 'Mail' icon. When the list email services come up, select one and follow the email setup instructions.

→ If you desire to link your email account to your Kindle Fire, enter your correct email and password.

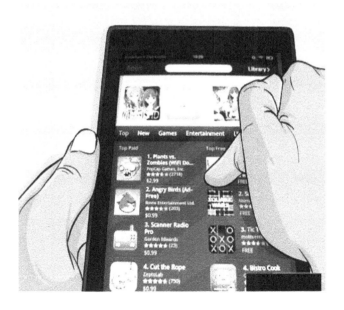

7. Other Apps and how to check them out:

In order to get available services and features that personalize your Kindle Fire HD to your preference, Select Home Icon → Apps → Store, to enable you open the Amazon App store.

→ As usual, purchasing most apps from the App store will cost some money, therefore remember to check the cost of the app before purchasing.

THE END